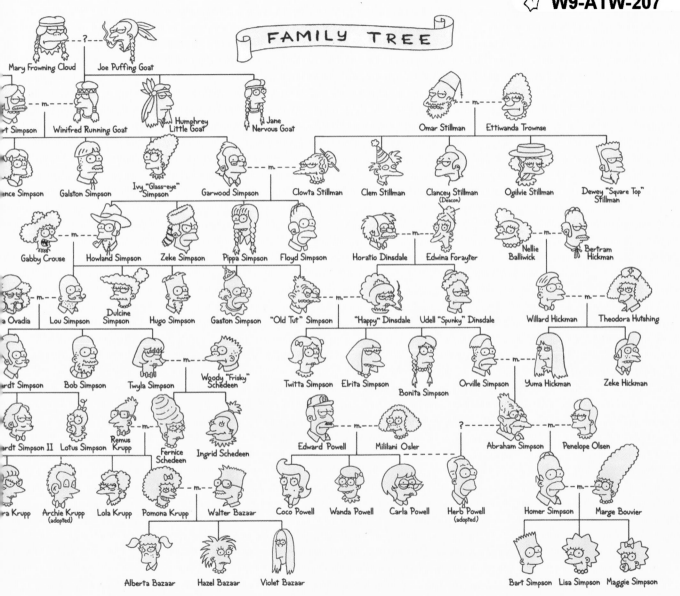

FAMILY TREE

Mary Frowning Cloud — Joe Puffing Goat

...rt Simpson — m — Winifred Running Goat — Humphrey Little Goat — Jane Nervous Goat

Omar Stillman — m — Ettiwanda Trownse

...nce Simpson — Galston Simpson — Ivy "Glass-eye" Simpson — Garwood Simpson — m — Clowta Stillman — Clem Stillman — Clancey Stillman (Deacon) — Ogilvie Stillman — Dewey "Square Top" Stillman

Gabby Crouse — m — Howland Simpson — Zeke Simpson — Pippa Simpson — Floyd Simpson — Horatio Dinsdale — m — Edwina Forayter — Nellie Balliwick — m — Bertram Hickman

...a Ovadia — m — Lou Simpson — Dulcine Simpson — Hugo Simpson — Gaston Simpson — "Old Tut" Simpson — m — "Happy" Dinsdale — Udell "Spunky" Dinsdale — Willard Hickman — m — Theodora Hutshing

...rdt Simpson — Bob Simpson — Twyla Simpson — m — Woody "Frisky" Schedeen — Twitta Simpson — Elrita Simpson — Bonita Simpson — Orville Simpson — m — Yuma Hickman — Zeke Hickman

...rdt Simpson II — Lotus Simpson — Remus Krupp — m — Fernice Schedeen — Ingrid Schedeen — Edward Powell — m — Mililani Osler — ? — Abraham Simpson — m — Penelope Olsen

...ra Krupp — Archie Krupp (adopted) — Lola Krupp — Pomona Krupp — m — Walter Bazaar — Coco Powell — Wanda Powell — Carla Powell — Herb Powell (adopted) — Homer Simpson — m — Marge Bouvier

Alberta Bazaar — Hazel Bazaar — Violet Bazaar

Bart Simpson — Lisa Simpson — Maggie Simpson

MATT GROENING'S

tHe SIMPSONS™

Uncensored Family Album

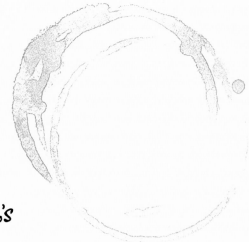

MATT GROENING'S

tHE SIMPSONS™

Uncensored Family Album

HARPER

NEW YORK • LONDON • TORONTO • SYDNEY

To Be Filed
1st PLACE SCIENCE FAIR
August 24, 1991
NATIONAL INFORMER
BIGFOOT!
SPRINGFIELD--Police here yesterday announced that they had captured and jailed Bigfoot, the elusive half-man, half-beast whose existence and evolutionary significance have been debated for decades by scientists and
August 25, 1991
NATIONAL INFORMER
ARRIED BIGFOOT!
SPRINGFIELD--With the eyes of the world riveted on this sleepy town, the amazing capture of Bigfoot took a bizarre turn yesterday when lifelong Springfield resident Marge Simpson alleged she had been married to the monster for the past 11 years.
Springfield Police Chief Wiggum said in a prepared statement, "All evidence seems to corroborate Ms. Simpson's assertion that the beast we captured yesterday is in fact her husband, Homer Simpson."
The couple, Ms. Simpson alleged, were on a camping trip
K-9 COLLEGE
"OBEDIENCE IS OUR BUSINESS"
DIAL 555-STAY
the Punjab Region, and I was stunned to say the very least. The gun man was not so funny despite his outfit."
laughing either as
chip rack near the
KWIK-E-MART OWNER APU
PLEASE!
IF FOUND, DROP IN ANY U.S. MAIL BOX
PLUTONIUM STORAGE ROOM
To Bert-
YOUR PAL, KRUSTY

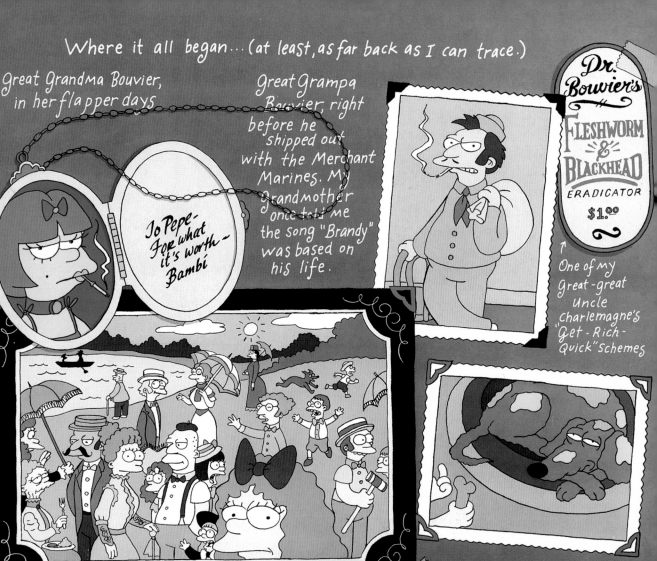

Where it all began... (at least, as far back as I can trace.)

Great Grandma Bouvier, in her flapper days

Great Grampa Bouvier, right before he shipped out with the Merchant Marines. My grandmother once told me the song "Brandy" was based on his life.

To Pepe - For what it's worth ~ Bambi

Dr. Bouvier's FLESHWORM & BLACKHEAD ERADICATOR $1.00

↑ One of my Great-great Uncle Charlemagne's "Get-Rich-Quick" Schemes

Bouvier Family Picnic, 1903

Great Grandma Bouvier's dog, Fetchy.

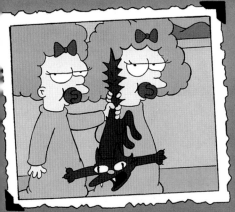

Patty and Selma in their infancy, with our cat, Squirmy.

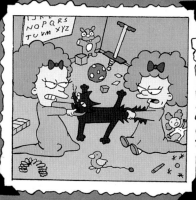

Patty, Selma (age 3½) and Squirmy.

Patty, Selma and me

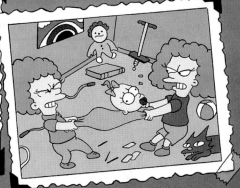

My first book! In the end, the Li'l Gnome grows to be 9 ft. tall. It taught me a valuable lesson about patience, hope and growth!

My first tooth

My second tooth

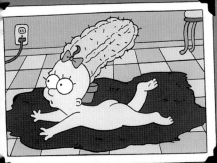

Little Marjorie Bouvier

OOH-WEE!

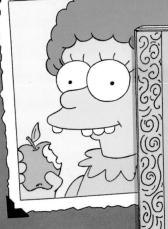

Despite my handicap, I won the kindergarten apple-bobbing contest.

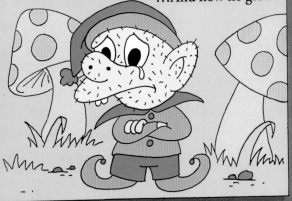

A "HEY, YOU! READ ME A STORY" BOOK

The **Fuzzy** Li'l **Gnome**

...And how he grew

At one time, my gum wrapper braid was 22 ft. long!

GUM
GOOEY
FRUI

CAVE OF DEPRESSION
NO SMOKING PLEASE!
NO SPITTING
NO PHOTOS
NO YELLING

Our family summer vacation. Dad said he wanted to "see America in all her splendor."

WORLD'S LARGEST
TIRE
8th WONDER OF THE WORLD!
EMPIRE TIR

My first attempt at creative expression (age 11½)

HONORABLE MENTION
STILL LIFE PHOTOGRAPHY

from the Capital City Daily Bugle!

What's smarter than a Spelling Bee?
DON'T MISS IT!
JOE
The Diving Pig!
NOTHIN' LIKE IT ON EARTH!
SEE HIM PERFORM LIVE DAILY! AT...
WATERWORLD
AQUATORIUM AND EXOTIC WARM WATER SEA PARK!
Plenty of Parking on Dry Land!
BUSES LEAVE DAILY!

Before

After

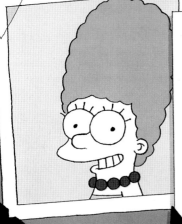

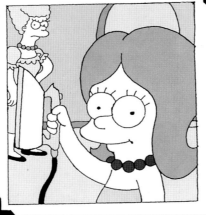

The day I straightened my hair (age 13).

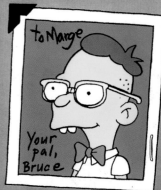

to Marge

Your pal, Bruce

My first boyfriend, Bruce Udelhofen

The Speech I Imagine JFK Would Have Made
At Our Graduation (Had He Lived)

My fellow citizens of Springfield High, the trumpet
summons us again to a long twilight struggle. The
torch has been passed to your generation and the
glow from that fire can truly light the campus.
So let us Begin.
Ich bin ein Springfielder!
ⅩⅩⅩⅩⅩⅩ   Ask not what you can do for Springfield High, but what Springfield High can do for you..

Other way around?

The first draft of my award-winning dramatic interpretation

Springfield High School
Certificate of Distinction

Awarded to: _Marge Bouvier_

In recognition of: _"Johnny, We Hardly Heard Ye"_

In the Category: _Dramatic Interpretation_

2nd Place   FORENSICS TEAM

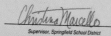
Supervisor, Springfield School District

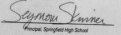
Principal, Springfield High School

Artie Ziff took first place with his poignant reading of "Don't Rain on My Parade", from "Funny Girl."

Grandpa Simpson's Army Days

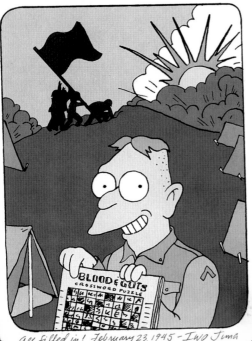

All filled in! February 23, 1945 - Iwo Jima

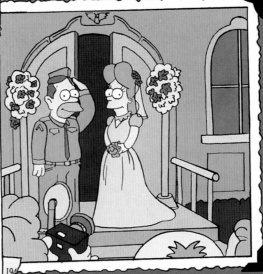

Grandma and Grandpa Simpson's wedding. I have them to thank for my dear Homer.

I found this in an old Almanac that Grandpa left in the bathroom♪

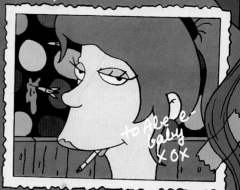

to Abe-e baby XOX

I don't know what her name was, but I do know that Homer's once-wealthy half-brother, Herb, was the result of their short-lived affair.

BLOOD & GUTS CROSSWORD PUZZLE

12) PFC. Harris
13) Sgt. Mulrooney
15) Extinct species of N. American shrubbery
16) Former Yugoslavian unit of currency
17) What Generals do in battle
19) _____ mobile
23) _____ Manchu
24) S. American tree fungus
25) Imitated
27) Jap
30) PFC. Richards
31) Lt. Richards
32) Two-toed Eurasian marsupial
34) PFC. Winoski

DOWN
1) Tasmanian flowering ragweed-(2 words)

11) PFC. O'Ryan
14) PFC. Di Nunzio
18) The entire 23rd platoon_____
20) Popular tune
21) Chinese root weevil
22) Nip
25) PFC. Roberts
26) Sgt. Gitman
33) "Stars _____ Stripes"

YOU SHOWED UP

Springfield Shopper
314 Dutch Elm St.
Springfield

Dear Shopper Editor,

I/We have had it up to here with your "news-paper" and it's reckless, anti-social policy of publishing story afterstory of babies being born, picture after picture of babies, advertisements of baby products, etc.

Where will it all end?

What about the rest of us who aren't not babies? Did it ever occur to you that we are the majority? If you ask me, you are only getting yourself in a real mess because the people will see all these babby stories and think "That's a good way to get my name in the paper," and that only leads to more babies!

So I'm ware warning you: if you continue this policy, I will see to it that no child of mine ever lays an eye on your publication.

Sicnerely,

Abraham Simpson

Abraham Simpson

P.S. If you don't think I'm serious, you should see my newborn son. He shows no interest in what your paper, or anything else for that matter, has to say. More power to him if you ask me!

Grandpa's first-recorded letter of complaint

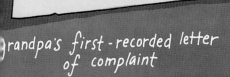

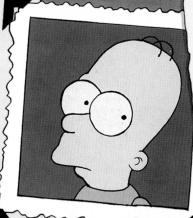

Little Homer Simpson, age 3 months

Grandpa's 7,587th oyster ↓

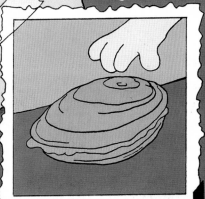

SHUCKS, He's the World's Best!

By Merl Merlow,
Shopper Business Editor

The Springfield Oyster Shucking Co. was all abuzz Friday with the news that

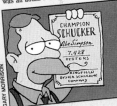

Abe Simpson

Abraham Simpson, 29, had hand-shucked 7,587 oysters between 8:00 Monday morning and 5:00 Friday afternoon.

Simpson's achievement surpassed the previous one-week record of 7,428, set by the late Lud "Load" Dennison in 1943.

"Not to take anything away from Lud or his beautiful widow," said an elated Abe Simpson when presented with a handsome scroll commemorating his feat, "but you have to remember that the Load set the record in a six-day work week during the war, when the only thing this place turned out was beef in a tin.

"I'd like to see [Dennison] try to break 5,000, let alone come close to my record, with big jumbos and those pretty little ones sailing down the conveyor belt. Now *that's* shuckin'."

Simpson said he planned to celebrate quietly at home with his 3-month-old son Homer.

"I'll probably just relax in front of the radio and try to get the smell off my hands," Simpson said.

In other business news... C. Montgomery Burns, 23, purchased the run down Springfield Gas and Electric Co., which has been closed for the past

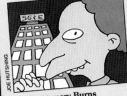

C. Montgomery Burns

five weeks. When asked whether he would reinstate the "Lights Out for the Weekend" campaign, Burns said,"By the time I'm through, there'll be enough power around here to light up four or five Springfields!"

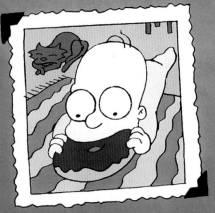

Homer always did have a fondness for donuts.

Grandpa and Homer in happier days.

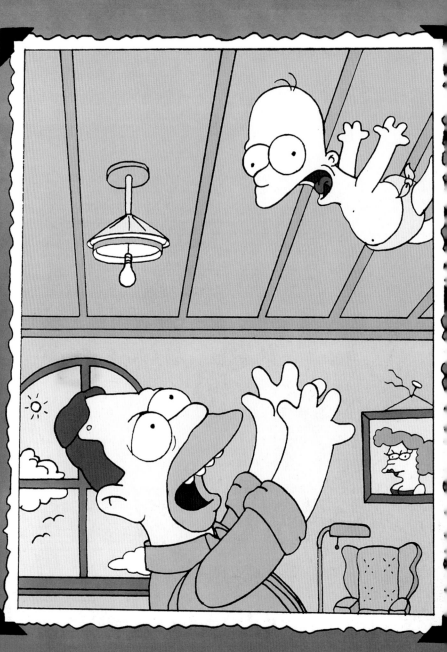

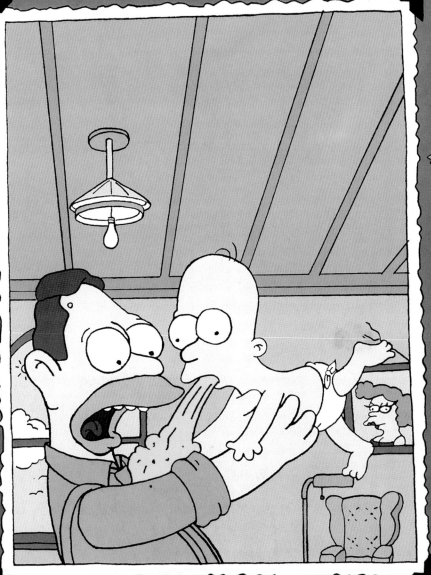

The first sign of Homer's budding intelligence. I can't really say his handwriting has improved much over the years.

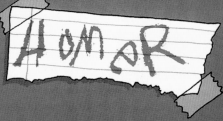

HomaR

The happier days were over quite quickly.

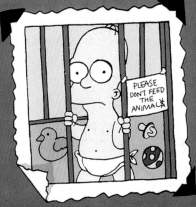

PLEASE DON'T FEED THE ANIMALS

SPRINGFIELD ELEMENTARY

"We mold young minds."
--Douglas Crone,
Ed D., Superintendent

Est. 1914

REPORT CARD

Simpson, Homer   GRADE   4

SUBJECT	1ST QUARTER	2ND QUARTER	3RD QUARTER	4TH QUARTER	SUMMER-SCHOOL
MATH	D	D	D-	D-	F
ENG	D+	D	D-	F+	F
HIST	D	D+	D+	D-	E
SCI	D-	D-	F	D	E
GYM	C-	C-	D	D+	D-
ATTEN-DANCE	F	D-	F	D-	F
CITIZEN-SHIP	F	D-	D-	F	D-

NOTES ~~We would like to hold Homer back a year, but his 4th grade teacher, Mrs. Harvell, has refused to take him back --HH~~

~~an insult to~~ ~~disruption~~ ~~underachie~~

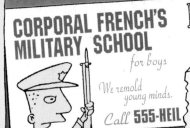

CORPORAL FRENCH'S MILITARY SCHOOL

for boys

We remold young minds.

Call **555-HEIL**

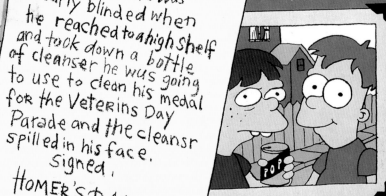

Our only photo of Herb Powell, Homer's once-wealthy half-brother.

Dear Principal Hartly,
Please excuse Homer's absince of Nov. 8-10. He had to stay home to look after his fathre, who was nearly blinded when he reached to a high shelf and took down a bottle of cleanser he was going to use to clean his medal for the Veterins Day Parade and the cleansr spilled in his face.
Signed,
HOMER'S DAD

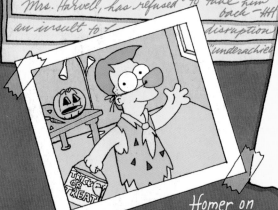

Homer on Halloween, in his all-time favorite costume. (age four)

Homer at the tender age of ten. That's Barney Gumble on the lef[t]

Dear Dad,
  I'll do anything you
say, just don't send
me to military
school. Please please
please please please
please please please
please please.
      Your devotid son,
                    Homer
P.S. Remember. Today is the
first day of the rest of your life.

AWARD
FOR EFFORT
Nice
WOODSHOP
Try

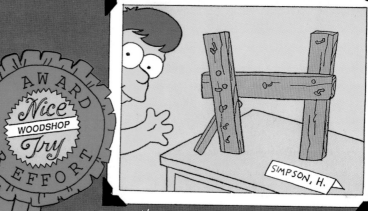

SIMPSON, H.

Homer's sophomore woodshop project—
his first initial. He planned to finish
the "J" as a junior and the "S"
as a senior.

FROM THE DESK OF
Harlan Dondelinger

To: Abraham Simpson

From: Harlan Dondelinger
      Vice Principal

Dear Mr. Simpson:
  I need to talk with you about ways to
improve Homer's study habits. His constant
efforts to draw attention to himself with
noises imitating bodily functions and his
off-color attempts at humor during class
time have reached the point where I have
no alternative but to warn you that
drastic measures may be necessary.
We've told him repeatedly that he's an
underachiever, but Homer seems to think
that's a compliment.

Sincerely,

Harlan Dondelinger
Vice Principal

← Yours truly!

Mrs. Harvell → 4th   SPRINGFIELD ELEMENTARY

Barney!

Mrs. Harvell

Principal Hartley

On prom night I wore my hair UP for the first time! A style that's never let me DOWN.
Betty's Beauty Barn
Specialzing in Unisex "NATURALS" For Men and Women Boys and Girls
(Yes, we groom dogs too!)
SPRINGFIELD HIGH SCHOOL AUDITORIUM "Goodbye Yellow Brick Road" CLASS OF '74 Senior Prom ADMIT ONE "It's your most special night ...behave yourselves"
SPRINGFIELD HIGH SCHOOL AUDITORIUM "Goodbye Yellow Brick Road" CLASS OF '74 Senior Prom ADMIT ONE "It's your most special night ...behave yourselves"
Senior Prom
CLASS OF 74
INGFIELD H.S.
GOODBYE YELLOW BRICK ROAD PROM
CAP'N RENO'S CREAMED SEAFOOD STEAM TABLE RESTARAUNT
YES! WE HAVE FROZEN MAINE LOBSTERS!
...BURGER
THE SPRINGFIELD
Artie Ziff and I went to dinner here after the prom and before that ugly incident at Inspiration Point. Men are such animals!

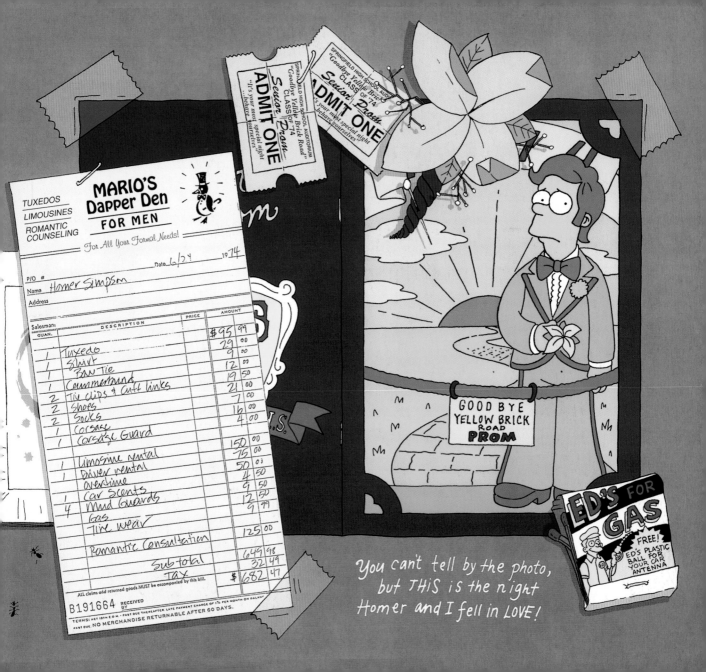

You can't tell by the photo, but THIS is the night Homer and I fell in LOVE!

KARMEL KORN
Enjoy the Movie!
Visit the Snack Bar!
DO NOT ATTEMPT TC CHEW UNPOPPED KORN KERNELS.
WE CANNOT BE RESPONSIBLE FOR
BROKEN TEETH OR DENTAL WORK OF ANY KIND.
From when I saw "The Love People" for the 8th time! I wept openly during the deathbed sequence every time!
My Hero!
LIVE!
IT'S A FAR OUT HAPPENING
IN A LUNCH TIME CONCERT!
THE LARRY DAVIS EXPERIENCE
IN THE
SPRINGFIELD HIGH
MULTI-PURPOSE ROOM
Thursday, April 12, 1973
Noon til 12:27
WARNING: PLEASE DO NOT REMOVE FLYERS FROM SCHOOL NOTICE BOARDS
à mon cher Homer- L'amour, Marge
The first and last pack of cigarettes I ever bought
LADY Laramie
HI-TAR
"you'll love 'em, Lady!"
Patty and Selma still smoke them!

HANDWRITING ANALYSIS

Your Personality Revealed Through Penmanship!

SIGNATURE *Marge Bouvier*

Your signature indicates a sensitive, free-spirited and creative nature. The graceful calligraphic curvatures of your capital letters reveal a love of poetry and music. You are destined for a life of elegance, refinement and artistic fulfillment.

SIGNATURE **HOMER SIMPSON**

Your signature exhibits a strong tendency toward slackness, inattention and woolgathering. The unsophisticated arrangement of ill-formed lines and circles which comprise your writing suggests an obtuse and insipid outlook. You are doomed to a life of banality, dullness and lethargy.

ROSES ARE RED
VIOLETS ARE
BLUE NO ONE
I KNOW
SPEAKS FRENCH
AS BEAUTIFULLY
AS YOU.
L'AMOUR,
HOMER

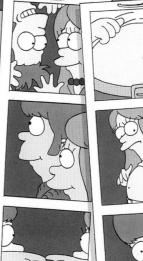

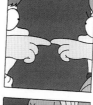

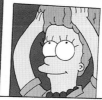

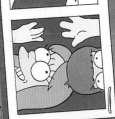

My 10 favorite Bands of All time, 1973

1. Ringo Starr
2. The Beatles
3. The Larry Davis Experience
4. The Happies
5. Elf Gravy
6. Don Donnally and Jo-Jo
7. Beatlemania
8. The Twigs of Sister Tomorrow
9. The Love Buckets
10. Mr. Funky and the Springfieldians

R.S. + M.B.

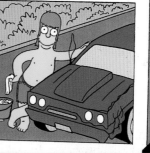

Homer's other love —
his car
← Such fond memories!

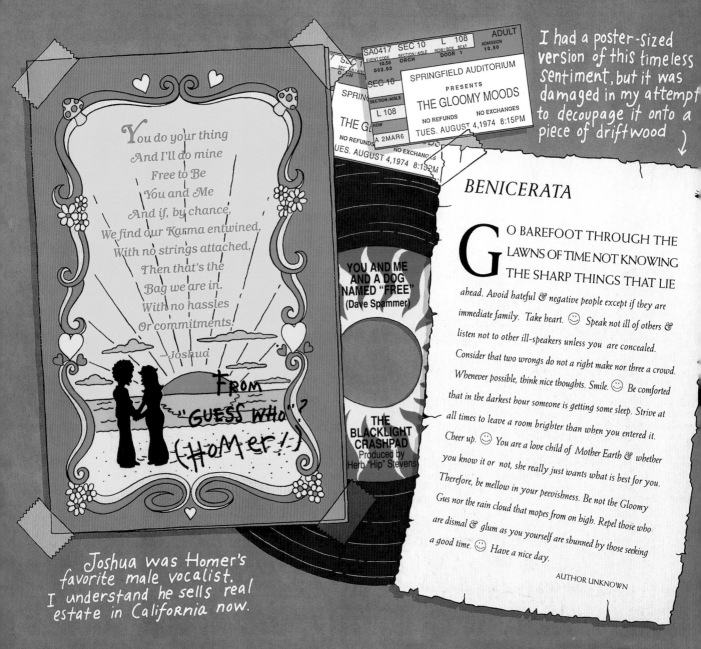

You do your thing
And I'll do mine
Free to Be
You and Me
And if, by chance,
We find our Karma entwined,
With no strings attached,
Then that's the
Bag we are in.
With no hassles
Or commitments.

—Joshua

FROM "GUESS WHO"? (HoMeR!)

Joshua was Homer's favorite male vocalist. I understand he sells real estate in California now.

SA0417 SEC 10 L 108 ADULT
EVENT CODE SECTION / AISLE ROW/BOX SEAT ADMISSION
10.50 ORCH 10.50
002.00 DOOR 1

SPRINGFIELD AUDITORIUM
PRESENTS
THE GLOOMY MOODS
NO REFUNDS NO EXCHANGES
TUES. AUGUST 4, 1974 8:15PM

I had a poster-sized version of this timeless sentiment, but it was damaged in my attempt to decoupage it onto a piece of driftwood ↓

YOU AND ME AND A DOG NAMED "FREE"
(Dave Spammer)

THE BLACKLIGHT CRASHPAD
Produced by Herb "Hip" Stevens

BENICERATA

GO BAREFOOT THROUGH THE LAWNS OF TIME NOT KNOWING THE SHARP THINGS THAT LIE ahead. Avoid hateful & negative people except if they are immediate family. Take heart. ☺ Speak not ill of others & listen not to other ill-speakers unless you are concealed. Consider that two wrongs do not a right make nor three a crowd. Whenever possible, think nice thoughts. Smile. ☺ Be comforted that in the darkest hour someone is getting some sleep. Strive at all times to leave a room brighter than when you entered it. Cheer up. ☺ You are a love child of Mother Earth & whether you know it or not, she really just wants what is best for you. Therefore, be mellow in your peevishness. Be not the Gloomy Gus nor the rain cloud that mopes from on high. Repel those who are dismal & glum as you yourself are shunned by those seeking a good time. ☺ Have a nice day.

AUTHOR UNKNOWN

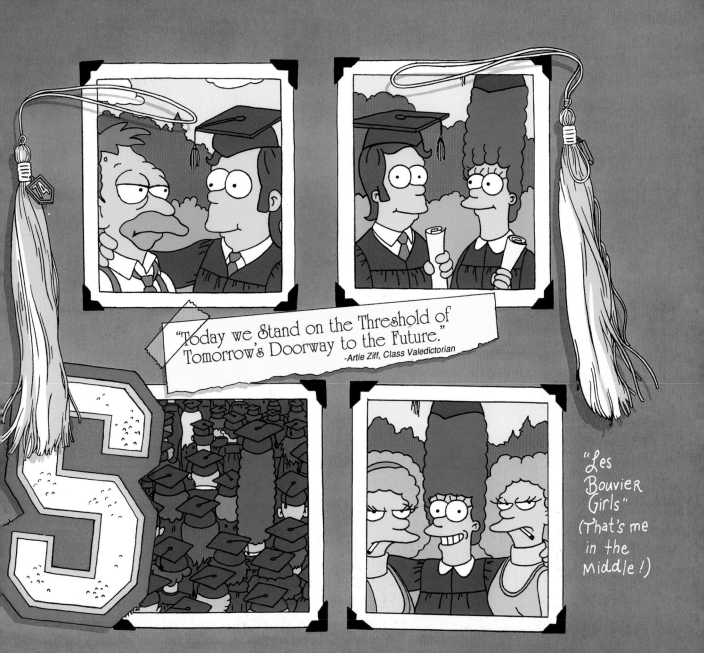

"Today we Stand on the Threshold of Tomorrow's Doorway to the Future."
-Artie Ziff, Class Valedictorian

"Les Bouvier Girls" (That's me in the middle!)

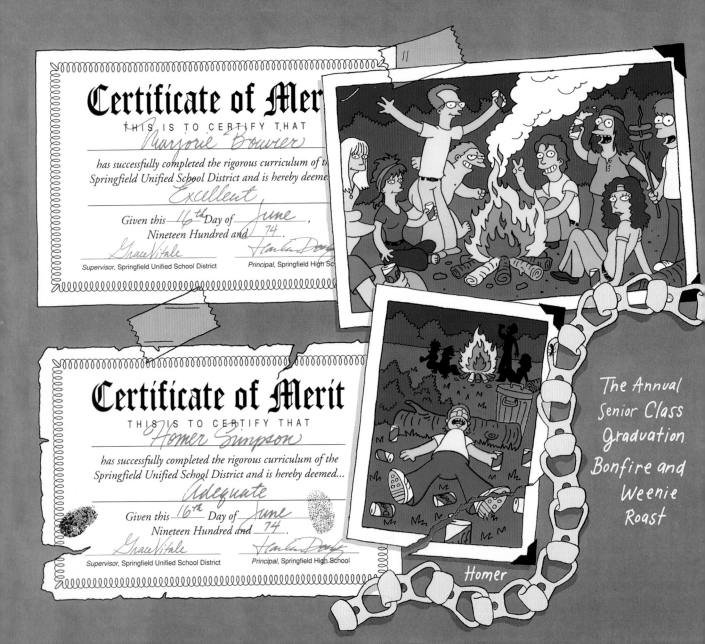

Certificate of Mer[it]

THIS IS TO CERTIFY THAT

Marjorie Bouvier

has successfully completed the rigorous curriculum of t[he] Springfield Unified School District and is hereby deeme[d]...

Excellent

Given this 16th Day of June, Nineteen Hundred and 74.

Grace Vitale
Supervisor, Springfield Unified School District

Principal, Springfield High Sch[ool]

Certificate of Merit

THIS IS TO CERTIFY THAT

Homer Simpson

has successfully completed the rigorous curriculum of the Springfield Unified School District and is hereby deemed...

Adequate

Given this 16th Day of June, Nineteen Hundred and 74.

Grace Vitale
Supervisor, Springfield Unified School District

Principal, Springfield High School

The Annual
Senior Class
Graduation
Bonfire and
Weenie
Roast

Homer

KZMK

Cosmic Radio for a More Cosmic Springfield!

WIN A Trip to Beautiful

HAWAII

JUST BY SENDING US YOUR TOP 10 DESERT ISLAND 8-TRACK CARTRIDGES!

1) ~~"Baby, Don't Get All Bent out of Shape" - the New Wunkies~~
2) ~~"Feelin' Kinda Bummed Out" - Joshua~~
3) ~~"Greatest Hits, Vol. 2" - the Larry Davis Experience~~
4) ~~"Jesus Was a Hippie" - Original Broadway Cast~~
5) ~~"Hung Up in Your Macrame" - The Gloomy Moods~~
6) ~~"Outta Sight, Inna Daze" - Cosmic Consciousness, Inc.~~
7) ~~"My Live-in Lady Love" - John Colorado~~
8) ~~"A decade of Opening Acts" - One Horse Stagecoach~~
9) ~~"Just Doin' my Thing," Vol. 3 - Joshua~~
10) ~~"Also Sprach Zarathustra" - The Electric Orange Dirigible~~

Name: Homer Simpson

Address: 37 1/2 E. Street, Springfield

* 3 Days and 2 Nights at the exotic Poi Lanai Motel, located on the secluded Island of Koolawe. Air fare not included.

In our wacky days!

(See Inside Front Cover for Details)
NUCLEAR POWER PLANTS
working in...
BIG PAY!
STEP UP TO
YOU CAN
NEXT TO MEL'S WATERBEDS AND POSTERS EMPORIUM
"DIG" THE "SCENE" AT...
THE LAVA-LAMP A-GO-GO!
SPRINGFIELD'S "GROOVIEST" DISCO!

A souvenir from when Homer and I were "swinging singles"!

Homer's Lucky tee

I DIDN'T KNOW they created A tribute to Dad at Sir Putt-A-Lots

HOLE #9

Your father was such a poet in his younger days.
IF EVER A MAN LOVED a WOMAN, I LOVE YOU MARGE. YOU ARE THE MOST WONDERFUL PERSON IN THE WORLD, AND I WILL BE THE LUCKIEST IF YOU AGREE TO BE MY WIFE.
Lucky 7 Wedding Chapel
NO Shoes
NO Shirt
NO Service!
VISIT our Craps Tables and Slot Machines!
OPEN 24 Hours!
NO REFUNDS!
Call 555-BWED
(FOR DIVORCE APPOINTMENTS, DIAL 555-BGON)
My lace garter belt
One of the happiest days of my life!
ME TOO!
(HOMer)
me 3 (BART)
WOODEN NICKEL 50¢ CASINO
WOODEN NICKEL 25¢ CASINO
Poker chip tokens compliments of the Lucky 7 Chapel
Our complimentary wedding rice (the bag cost extra).
aye CARUMBA!

Marriage Certificate

THIS DOCUMENT CERTIFIES ___Marge Bouvier___

AND ___Homer Simpson___ TO BE UNITED IN HOLY

MATRIMONY ON THE ___29___ DAY OF ___September___

BY THE POWERS VESTED (BY LAW) IN A JUSTICE OF THE

PEACE, AT THE ___Lucky 7 Wedding Chapel___

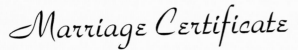

Milford A. Alexander
Justice of the Peace

Doris Troy
Clerk

OFFICIAL

"*May your marriage not be a lemon.*"

*Our favorite casino!
Such lovely
memories!*

The WOODEN NICKEL Saloon & Casino

HEY-
WHAT HAVE
YOU GOT
TO LOSE?!

THE TOMB OF THE UNKNOWN HITCH-HIKER

A Public Service Cautionary Statue

*This grim monument is located on a particularly
desolate stretch of highway not far from the Lucky 7.*

For the Tub of Your Life
KUSTOM-KRAFTED SPAS AND HOT TUBS

○ **Nathen "Red" Wood** ○
"Not 'Just Another' Spa & Hot Tub Salesman"
24 Hour Beeper: 1-800-555-9007

*We met this nice
man while playing keno.
I found it hard to believe
he was in such a risqué
line of work!*

DEAR Ringo,

I hope you like this paINTING I DID
oF you. You are my favorite musician in
the universe (really!)

What do you like to eat?
Is your hair really that shape all the time?
Do you have hamburgers and French fries
in England?

Well, that's all for now. Please write me
you have time in your very busy schedule.

Yours truly,

Your biggest fan,

Marge Bouvier :)

Marge Bouvier

(P.S. I am
not a
lunatic.)

SPRINGFIELD THIRD PLACE FAIR

Lucky Coin Gelatin Mold
(whoever gets the coin is Lucky for a day!)

2 packs blue gelatin mix

3 cups "Krusty Brand" corn
sweetener

1 lb. bag multi-colored
"Kitchen Dee-Lite" miniature
marshmallows

1 Lucky coin (for chefs on a budget,
pennies are acceptable. For special
events, try using a Bicentennial
quarter.)

My secret ingredient:

Fla...

Boil gelatin i...
Pour into m...
Add marshm...
Chill for...

Voila!

SPRINGFIELD GELATIN COOK-OFF

BOUVIER   THIRD PLACE

August   1980

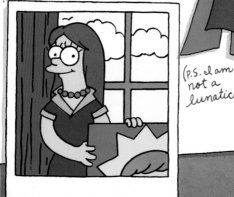

For this prize-winning mold, I used an Indian-head nickel! ↑

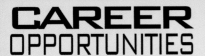

SPRINGFIELD NUCLEAR POWER PLANT

EMPLOYEE EVALUATION SHEET

Complete the Sentence: The most important thing for any worker is: _____

to try NOT TO LET THE SAME SONG KEEP RUNNING THROUGH YOUR HEAD

Behind my back, friends say I'm: ~~An EASY WORTH KNOWING~~ BRAVE, CLEAN AND REVEREND.

APPROVED

My ideal dinner would be: Smothered WITH COUNTRY GRAVY.

Hom

page 12

S.N.P.P. IDENTIFICATION CARD

1976

NAME: SIMPSON, HOMER

CLASS: SECTOR D

00876-54779-4

Homer Simpson

OUR MOTTO: A Tense Workplace is a Productive Workplace

NUCLEAR POWER IS OUR BEST FRIEND

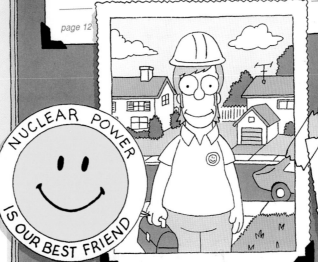

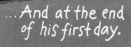

Homer on the morning of his first day of work as a *Power Plant* employee!

...And at the end of his first day.

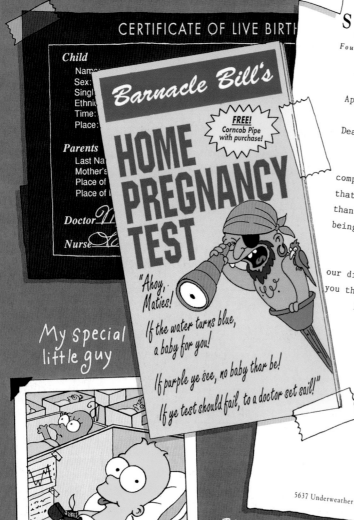

CERTIFICATE OF LIVE BIRTH

Child
Name:
Sex:
Singl
Ethnic
Time:
Place:

Parents
Last Na
Mother's
Place of
Place of

Doctor
Nurse

Barnacle Bill's
HOME PREGNANCY TEST

FREE! Corncob Pipe with purchase!

"Ahoy, Maties!

If the water turns blue, a baby for you!

If purple ye see, no baby thar be!

If ye test should fail, to a doctor set sail!"

My special little guy

It was awfully nice of them to keep Bart in a private room for the rest of the afternoon.

SPRINGFIELD GENERAL HOSPITAL
Founded 1925   Established 1926

April 2

Dear Mr. and Mrs. Simpson,

After careful consideration and in view of complaints registered by other parents, we must ask that you remove your son from the hospital no later than 5 p.m. today, so that we may ensure the well-being of the other newborns.

As you usher baby Bert into the world, Dr. Mizzell, our director of maternity, has asked me to convey to you the following wish:

Don't bring him back.

Sincerely,

Hilda Beck

Hilda Beck, R.V.N.
Director of Nursing

"Your illness is our business."

5637 Underweather Blvd., Springfield   Right across from the Burns Memorial Golf Course.

CIGAR
EXPLO-DO
BE THE LI THE F
THEY REALLY EXPLODE

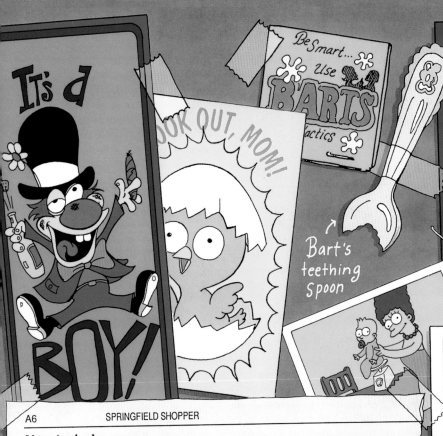

Bart's teething spoon

We were so proud!
(And still are!)

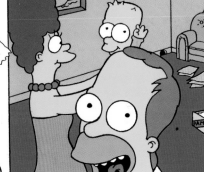

The Happy Family!

New Arrivals

WELCOME
Justinian Toby Carson of Springfield. A robust 8 pounds 4 ounces of All-American Boy, and no April Fool! Congratulations from your gushing grandparents—Libby, Big Bill, Viv and Captain Jack.

AIN'T SHE SWEET?!
Ashley Tiffany Hurley Born March 30 to Joe Don and Raelene Hurley of Springfield. Younger than springtime by nine days, honey, but you'll catch up soon enough. From your cousins Jim Bob, Erlene and Buford of Capital City, where all of us Hurleys are in a real hurry to meet you.

TROUBLE AHEAD!
Bartholomew J. Simpson Born April 1 to Homer and Marjorie Simpson of Springfield. A mere 7 pounds 5 ounces of spon- taneous combustion, but look what that one little cow did to Chicago. Marge, don't say we didn't warn you. Your loving sisters are close by in case 911 is busy. Patty and Selma. P.S. We saw Artie Ziff the other day and he asked after you. Such a nice boy.

EGG DROP!
Huong Kim Nguyen Born April 2 to Nguyen and Thu Nguyen of Springfield. Especially for you, little Nguyen, a birthday haiku:

Lotus child, welcome.
It's a small world after all.
Springfield, have a cow!

From your auntie Kim Tran.

SPRINGFIELD GENERAL HOSPITAL

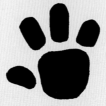

Name: Simpson, Bartholomew

Parents: Marge/Homer

Date: April 1st

Weight: 7.2 lbs.

Length: 19.0" Sex: M

Delivering Physician:

Dr. Julius Hibbert

Homer's →

← Mine

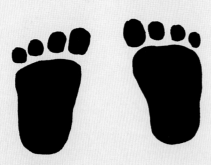

My first grey hair
(and hopefully my
last!) ↓

SPRINGFIELD GENERAL HOSPITAL

CLAIMS DEPT.

We regret to inform you that unless the outstanding balance shown below is paid in full by September 15, we will have no alternative but to repossess your child.

Delivery and Maternity Care
Bartholomew J. Simpson
Balance Due: $1,499.99

FINAL NOTICE

BARTHOLOMEW J SIMP

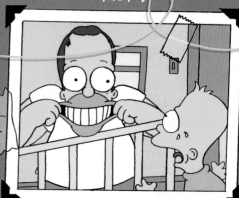

I was so thrilled when the doctor announced:
"four toes on each foot, four fingers on each hand."

Bart and Lisa's first Haircuts.

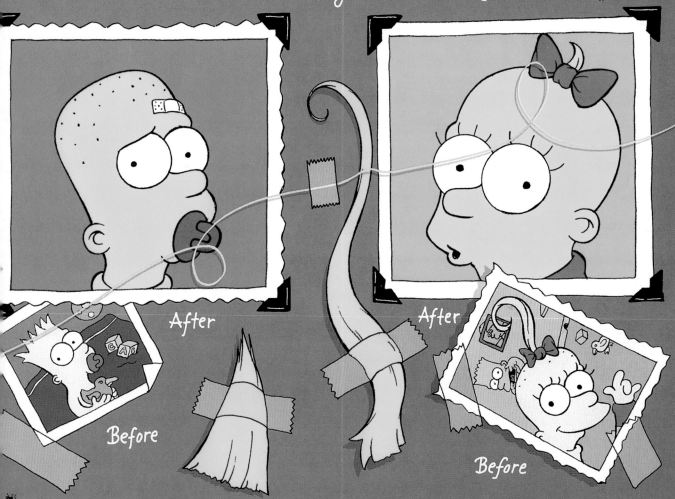

After

Before

After

Before

Lisa's hair never quite grew back the same.

Spend the night with
ELVISH
(EL-VEESH´)

ELVISH 'N' KABOB!

"THE TURKISH ELVIS"
Enjoy a Most Intimate Spectacle!
An incredible life-like simulation of an actual
Elvis concert re-enactment!
Live, on stage four times a night, seven days a week!

"I get deja-vu everytime I see it!" - Cliff Wilkins
The Town Crier

HUNKA HUNKA BURNIN' KABOB!
Special Dinner 'n' Show Combo.............$27.50
(Includes salad, rolls & choice of beverage or butter)

SIX DRINK MINIMUM **ONE**

SIX DRINK MINIMUM **ONE**

We spent
the night with
ELVISH

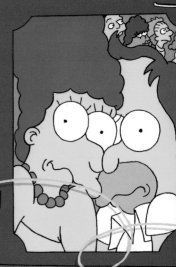

$17.95 for this STUPID PICTURE!
THEY GET YOU DRUNK THEN THEY
TAKE YOUR MONEY!

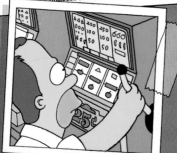

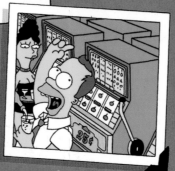

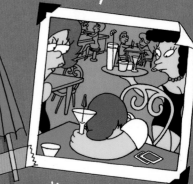

Homer at the slots.
He kept saying he "felt lucky", so I couldn't stop him.

Jackpot!

Homer after
he lost the entire
$11,158.97

Springfield kindergarten
REPORT CARD

Name: *SIMPSON, LISA*
Teacher: *MRS. WELLSLEY*

Alphabet	A
Storytime	A
Cookies & Milk Time	A
	B
Recess	A
Songtime	A
Numbers	A

Mrs. Simpson,
Lisa is a bright
and introspective
child. The word
"gifted" may be
applicable.
Although perhaps
she is too
introspective
and gifted for
her own good.
Mrs. Wellsley

BART - AGE 8

Bart's first black eye.
(and not his last, I'm
afraid.)

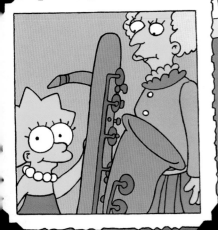

LISA with her kindergarten
teacher, Mrs. Wellsley.
(and her baritone Sax) Age 5.

I had a cat named
Snowball --
She died! She died!
Mom said she was
sleeping --
She lied! She lied!
Why oh why is my
cat dead?
Couldn't that Chrysler
hit me instead?
- Lisa Simpson

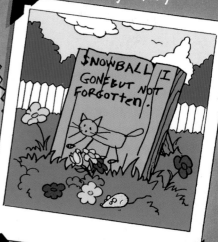

SNOWBALL I
GONE BUT NOT
FORGOTTEN.

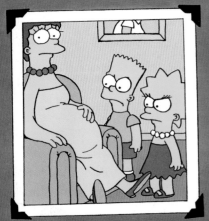

Here I am pregnant with Little Maggie!

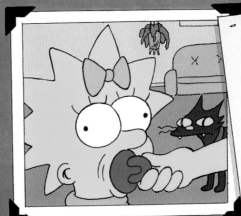

Maggie was such an easy child! By the time she came along, I knew all the tricks!

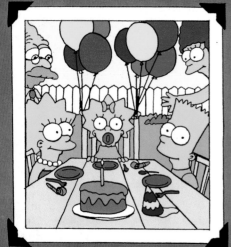

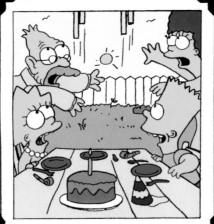

Maggie's First Birthday

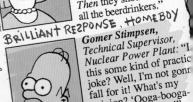
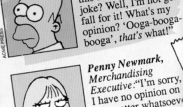

I was so, so, so proud! ↓

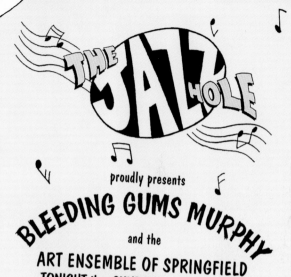

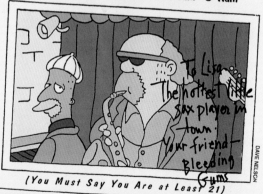

To Lisa— The hottest little sax player in town. Your friend— Bleeding Gums

(You Must Say You Are at Least 21)

DAVE NELSON

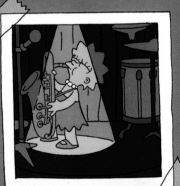

I don't know much about this man's music, but I do wish he'd do something about that name!

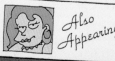

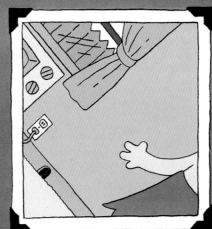
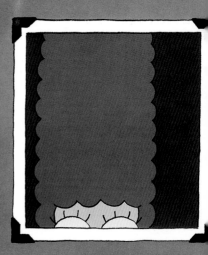

The Day Homer Got His New Camera

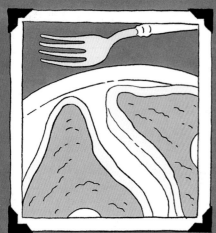
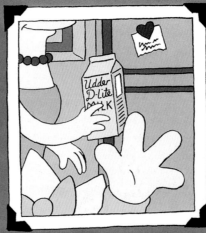
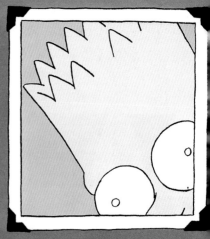

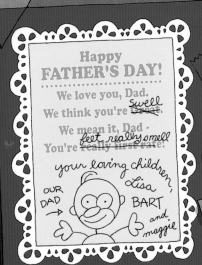

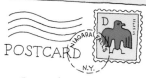

Our "Second Honeymoon"!

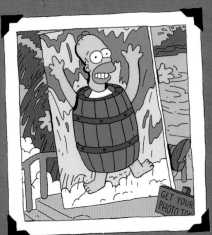

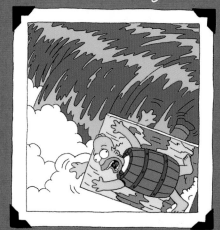

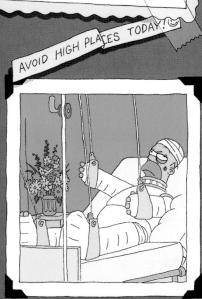

(Cut short by a most unfortunate accident.)

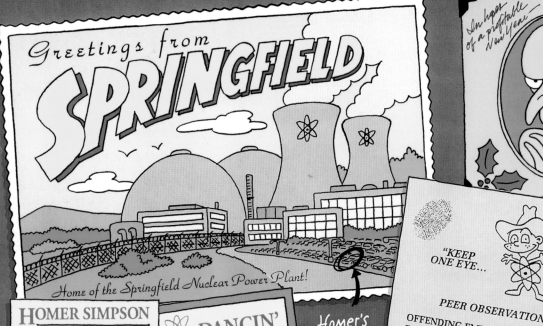

Greetings from **SPRINGFIELD**

Home of the Springfield Nuclear Power Plant!

In hopes of a profitable New Year—

I'm watching you—
C. Montgomery Burns

Homer's Car!

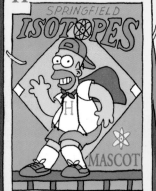

HOMER SIMPSON

SPRINGFIELD
ISOTOPES

H

MASCOT

DANCIN' HOMER SIMPSON

Took the baseball world by surprise in May 1990 when his spontaneous "Baby Elephant Walk" routine during Family Night became the talk of Springfield... Popular appeal earned him a shot at the majors, but "Walk" failed to catch on with Capital City fans...Among mascots, shares record (with several others) for shortest major league career.

HEIGHT: 5'9"   **WT:** 239 lbs.   **AGE:** 35

LITTLE KNOWN FACT: Homer was named Springfield Nuclear Power Plant "Toxic Waste Handler of the Month" in November, 1986.

A Simpson on a trading card — I never thought I'd see the day!

"KEEP ONE EYE...   ON THE OTHER GUY."

PEER OBSERVATION PROGRAM

OFFENDING EMPLOYEE: Homer Simpson
DATE OF OFFENSE: 8-4-85
TIME OF OFFENSE: all Day

Feel free to check as many offenses as you like. Every effort will be made to keep accuser's name confidential, but management cannot be responsible for leaked information.

EMPLOYEE HAS BEEN SEEN OR HEARD:

✓ taking a nap of more than 15 minutes while opperationg equipment

✓ taking fissionable matieral home for personal use

✓ taking Mr. Burns' name in vain

✓ taking liberties

___ other (use back of card to describe)

SIGNED (optional): anonymous

Thank you for helping make the plant more productive.

(Please do not fill out this form on company time.)

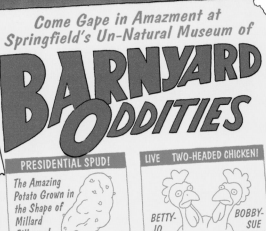

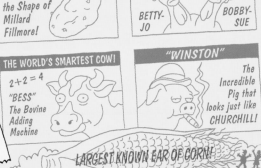

The ticket Homer refused to pay. He said it was a "principal thing" and hung it on the refrigerator.

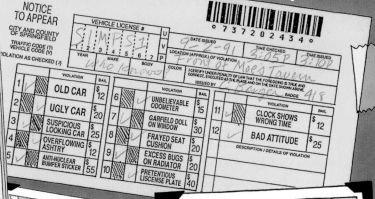

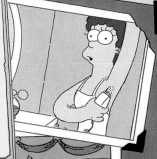

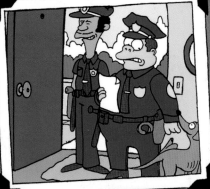

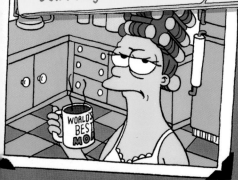

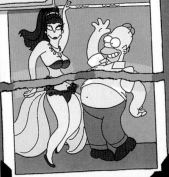

So later, Police Chief Wiggum and Eddie had to serve Homer with a warrant.

So much for matters of principal!

MOTH

Bart's tattoo. What a frightening experience! We had it removed immediately.

Needless to say, it bounced.

BARNEY GUMBEL
466 Prunetree Ln.
Springfield
00249
Saturday, 1990
Pay ONE MILLION DOLLARS and 00/100
to the Order of HOMER SIMPSON
FIRST NATIONAL BANK OF SPRINGFIELD, MAIN BRANCH
For BAR BET
Barney Gumbel

SUNDAY BOB PICKER'S
AMERICA, U.S.A.
NUCLEAR WARHEAD MUSEUM AND RELIGIOUS ARTS CENTER
FAT MAN
WAY 99 - EAST OF I-385

Ned and Maude F. sent us this one. On the back it reads: "Pray for peace, prepare for war, and vicey-versa!" That certainly is food for thought!

LIONEL HUTZ
ATTORNEY AT LAW
AS SEEN ON TV!
KLondike 5-LAWW
No Case Too Small!
Se Habla Espanol!
CLOGGING OUR COURTS SINCE 1976

Mambo your way to Happiness!
the Walt Bingham Way!
Even if you've got two LEFT feet, we'll put you on the RIGHT path! So...don't get LEFT behind! Start our classes RIGHT away before we fill up!

Quality Candles
1954 Burns Parkway
Springfield

Dear Sir or Madam:

   Correct me if I'm wrong, but I thought a person's 80th birthday was supposed to be a festive and dignified event.

   I don't seem to hear you correcting me.

   All right then, how do you suppose I felt when it was time to blow out the Quality (Hah! Now that's a hot one - if you get my meaning) Candle on my 80th birthday cake and I blew my damnedest and nothing happened. Oh, all right, maybe the flame did lean over a few degrees, but not so's you'd notice.

   Tell me this, Mr. or Ms. rocket scientist. If I made a wish, and the candle didn't go out, do I get a bonus wish? Well, if I do, here it is: I wish your whole ball of wax would go up in smoke!

                          Smoldering mad,
                          Abraham Simpson
                          Abraham Simpson

P.S. Have you ever thought about making half-size birth-day candles? It would save valuable time while honest people such as myself waited for the thing to burn to the ~~And another thing - how about chocolate-flavored~~ at pink stuff tastes awful!

NEW! GROUND ZERO LOTTERY
Scratch off 3 ☀ to win $1,000,000!

FISSION
FUSION

NEW! GROUND ZERO LOTTERY
Scratch off 3 ☀ to win $1,000,000! Scratch only 1 box from each row. Invalid if more than 3 boxes have been scratched. SCRATCH OFF 3 ONLY TO WIN!

FISSION
FUSION
SOLAR

Bart naked on a bear skin rug.

EL BARTO WAS HERE

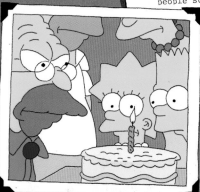

Grandpa's 80th Birthday

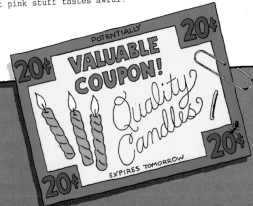

POTENTIALLY VALUABLE COUPON! *Quality Candles*
20¢ 20¢ 20¢ 20¢
EXPIRES TOMORROW

REPORT CA
Name: Santa's Little Helper
Owner: Simpson, Bart
1st Wk. 2nd Wk. 3rd Wk.
SIT F F F
STAY F F F
COME F F F
HEEL F F F
LIE DOWN F F F
SHAKE F F F
NO BEGGING F F F
Comments: I never would have admitted this before, but you can't teach some dogs new tricks!
EMILY WINTHROP'S K-9 COLLEG
He's trouble, but we love him.
PASS
Mrs. Simpson —
Your dog dug a huge trench through my Japanese Banzai garden. Some of the trees he killed were 140 years old!
SANTA'S LITTLE HELPER
555-8707

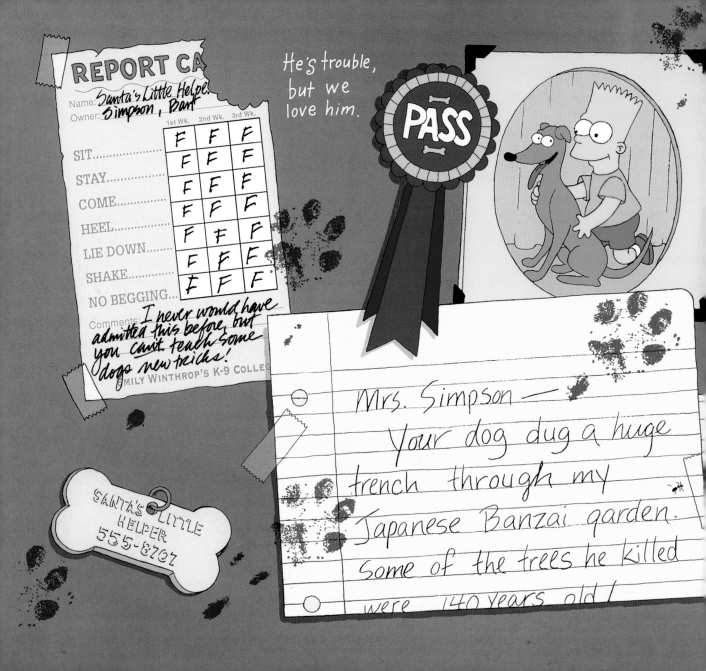

Dear Principal Skinne
Please excuse Bart's
absince from school
~~today~~, March 3-5. He
stayed home to take
care of his mother,
who could not use her
hands because she
burned both of them
in a Terrible Kitchen
accident, which is
why this letter looks
like a kid did it.

Sincerely,
Margorie Simpson
March 6th

SPRINGFIELD ELEMENTARY SCHOOL

March 6

Dear Mr. and Mrs. Simpson:

I know I've said this many times before, but this really is the last straw.

Enclosed you will find your son Bartholomew's latest pathetic attempt at forgery. If he thinks he can hoodwink my authority, he's got another think coming.

I'm afraid your son Bartholomew is on a one-way conveyor belt to J.D.H., and I don't mean the Junior Disneyland Hotel. I mean the Juvenile Detention Home!

I am adding another 40 days detention, which brings his total to 462 days.

He will also be required to write on the blackboard 1000 times:

A FORGED EXCUSE IS INEXCUSABLE.

I can only hope you will take even sterner measures of discipline in the privacy of your own home.

Sincerely,

Seymour Skinner

Seymour Skinner
Principal

SPRINGFIELD ELEME

REPORT CARD

SPRINGFIELD ELEMENTARY SCHOOL

tudent: Simpson, Bart

	1st SEM.	2nd SEM.	3rd SEM.
Arithmatic	F	D-	F
Social Studies	D+	F	F+
English	D-	F+	D
History	F	F	D-
Art	F-	D	D+
P.E.	D+	F	F

omments: Dear Mr. and Mrs. Simpson,
As we are painfully aware, Bart is his own worst enemy.
Unfortunately, the enemy is winning.
Nothing you or I could say or do would make a bit of difference.

With mutual concern,
Ms. Krabappel

rom the Desk of
. Loren Pryor
ISTRICT PSYCHOLOGIST

UBJECT: Bart Simpson Age: 10

VALUATION: Subject exhibits need to draw excessive attention to himself. Confrontational behavior includes attempts at raw humor intended to confuse authority figures and disrupt peer group order.

CONCLUSION: Rotten Little Punk.

SIGNED: J. Loren Pryor

EL BARTO WAS HERE

SPRINGFIELD ELEMENTARY
GRADE FOUR
Ms. Krabappel
Ms. Krabappel
Principal Skinner

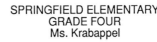

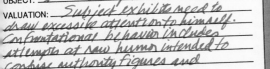

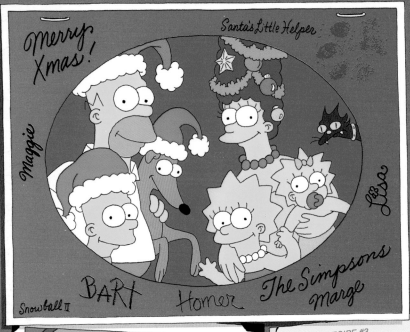

Merry Xmas!

Maggie

Santa's Little Helper

Snowball II   BART   Homer   The Simpsons   Marge   Lisa

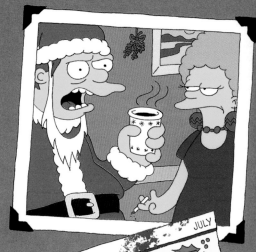

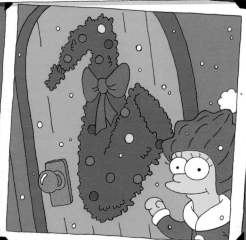

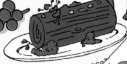

My Xmas List
Lisa

A pony
A pony
A pony
A pony
A pony
A pony
A pony

I don't know _what_ I'll do if I don't get a pony this year.

My Xmas List
Homer

- Stealth Bowler
- Coupon Booklet For Barney's Bowlarama
- NO TIES, please
- Case of Duff
- Mambo Refresher Course

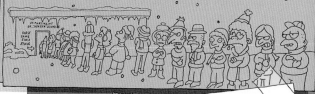

My Xmas List
Bart

tattoo - secret combo padlock for my bedroom door.
yoyo
ucer - MOON Shoes
- Electric RAZOR
- RADIO
full active Man walkie
rusty talkie
t-shirt
Space Mutants - Pop Gun

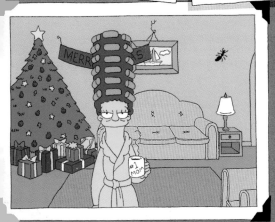

Xmas morning, 6:03 A.M.

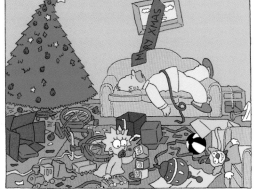

Xmas morning, 6:07 A.M.

Homer's first and last attempt at dental floss.

The Betsy Ross Mint
OFFICIAL FAMILY COAT OF ARMS

VENI VIDI VICI

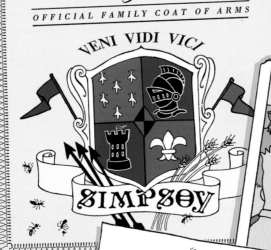

SIMPSOY

The Betsy Ross Mint
PURVEYORS OF FINE COLLECTIBLES SINCE 1972

Dear HOMER SIMPSOY,

We are delighted to inform you that due to the unique heritage of the SIMPSOY name, you have been selected to receive an authentic SIMPSOY family coat-of-arms.

This one-of-a-kind crest, prepared by the Betsy Ross Mint Collection's staff of trained genealogists, is officially documented and ~~registered~~ with the Society of Caucasian Heritage.

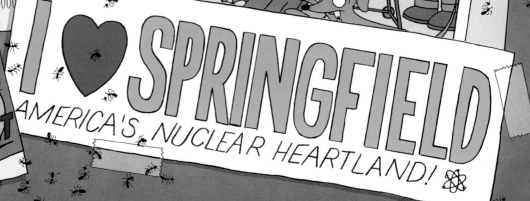

FLAV-R-PACKLET

I ♥ SPRINGFIELD
AMERICA'S NUCLEAR HEARTLAND!

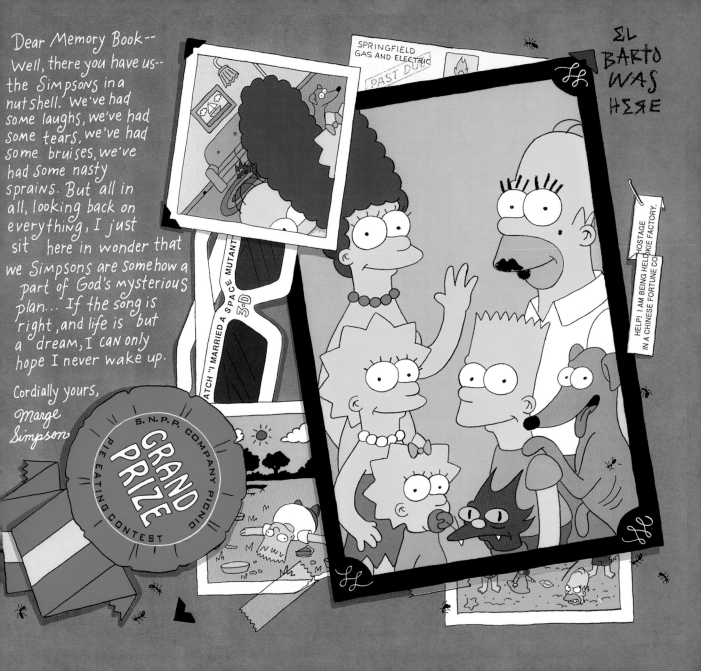

Dear Memory Book--
Well, there you have us--
the Simpsons in a
nutshell. We've had
some laughs, we've had
some tears, we've had
some bruises, we've
had some nasty
sprains. But all in
all, looking back on
everything, I just
sit here in wonder that
we Simpsons are somehow a
part of God's mysterious
plan... If the song is
right, and life is but
a dream, I can only
hope I never wake up.

Cordially yours,
Marge
Simpson

EL
BARTO
WAS
HƎЯE

SPRINGFIELD
GAS AND ELECTRIC
PAST DUE

S.N.P.P. COMPANY PICNIC
GRAND PRIZE
PIE EATING CONTEST

HELP! I AM BEING HELD HOSTAGE
IN A CHINESE FORTUNE COO...

WATCH "I MARRIED A SPACE MUTANT"
3-D

Dedicated to the memory of Snowball I:

We've re-upholstered the couch you shredded, but not our love for you.

The Simpsons™, created by Matt Groening, are the copyrighted and trademarked property of Twentieth Century Fox Film Corporation. Used with permission. All rights reserved. Originally published in 1991 by HarperCollins Publishers.

The Simpsons™ Uncensored Family Album.
Copyright © 1991, 2006 by Matt Groening Productions, Inc. All rights reserved. Printed in Singapore.
No part of this book may be used or reproduced in any manner whatsoever without written permission except in the case of brief quotations embodied in critical articles and reviews. For information address HarperCollins Publishers, 10 East 53rd Street, New York, NY 10022.

HarperCollins books may be purchased for educational, business, or sales promotional use. For information please write: Special Markets Department, HarperCollins Publishers, 10 East 53rd Street, New York, NY 10022.

First Harper paperback published 2006.

ISBN-10: 0-06-113830-4
ISBN-13: 978-0-06-113830-0

06 07 08 09 10 IM 10 9 8 7 6 5 4 3 2 1

Concept, Design, and Art Director: Mili Smythe
Design: Peter Alexander
Design Associate: Barbara McAdams
Family Album Chroniclers: Mary Trainor, Ted Brock
Chronicle Contributor: Jamie Angell
Creative Team: John Adam, Dale Hendrickson, Ray Johnson,
Bill Morrison, Willardson & Associates
Production Assistance: Kim Llewellyn, Dan Chavira
Typesetting: Skil-Set Graphics
Legal Advisor: Susan Grode
Editor: Wendy Wolf

THE BOUVIERS
Victor Bouvier
m.
Florette DuChamps
Claire DeLune
m.
Jean-Paul LaValle
Simone LaValle
Charmaine Renault
m.
Bernard DeBoeuf
Victor "Hugo" Bouvier II
m.
Gabrielle Gateau
Lili "Chou-Chou" LaValle
Georges LaValle
Coco LaValle
Diana LaValle
m.
Horst DeBoeuf
Honoré Bouvier
Didi Bouvier
Yves "Gauche" Bouvier
m.
Hermès DuLac
m.
Eva DeBoeuf
Zsa Zsa DeBoeuf
Bébé DeBoeuf
Mignon DeBoeuf
m.
Philippe Billout
Cléo Bouvier
Théo Bouvier
Fr. René
Louis DuLac
Marie "La Coquille" St. Jacques
m.
Henri Petitbois
Françoise Billout
m.
Antoine Bouvier
Jacques Bouvier
Alvarine Bisque
m.
Ferdinand Gurney
Bambi Petitbois
m.
Pépé Bouvier
Monique Bouvier
(Twins)
Lalique Bouvier
Fifi Bouvier
Coquette Bouvier
m.
Ingrid Gurney
m.
Clancy Bouvier
Charlene Bouvier
JoJo Bouvier
Chester Bouvier
m.
Alfreda LeDoux
Theodore "Teddy" L'eau
Hi L'eau
Tilda L'eau
Homer Simpson
m.
Marge Bouvier
Patty Bouvier
Selma Bouvier
Dotty Bouvier
Tootsie Bouvier
Rowena Bouvier
Alfreda Bouvier II
Pierre Bouvier
m.
Miranda Potter
Bart Simpson
Lisa Simpson
Maggie Simpson
Axel Bouvier
(Father Unknown)
Dolly Bouvier
Lolly Bouvier
Polly Bouvier

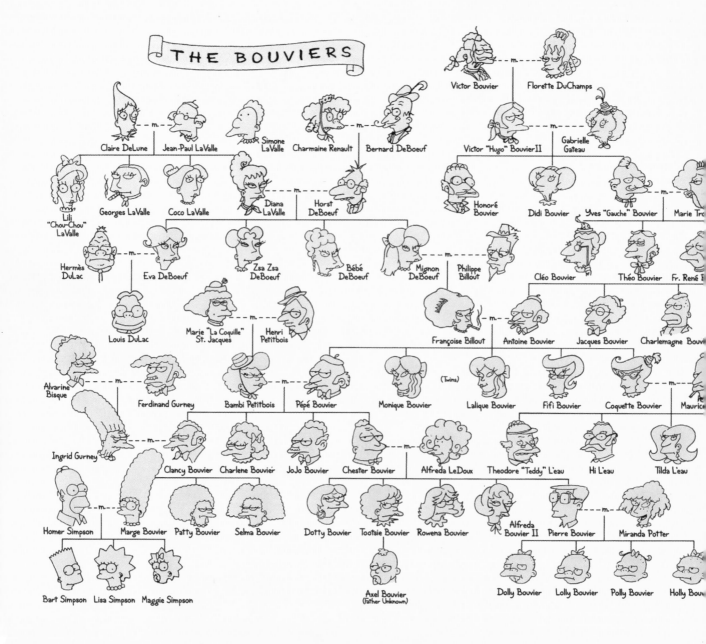